Dipping
into Hope
An Anchor in
Stormy Waters

Alan Hilliard

ISBN: 978 1 7881 2721 9

Typeset in Adobe Garamond Pro and The Seasons
Design by Brendan McCarthy
Printed by GPS Colour Graphics
Cover image: Shutterstock.com
Interior images: Alan Hilliard

Messenger M̄JP Publications

Milltown Park, Dublin D06 W9Y7,
Ireland
www.messenger.ie

Dedication

I'd like to dedicate this book to all those who made me feel welcome in the parish of City Quay and the parishes of Westland Row and University Church. Thanks also to those I share time with in the National Maternity Hospital, Holles St, and all at St Andrews Resource Centre, Pearse St. You all bring me hope each and every day. Please believe that you do this for me and others and continue to do this great work.

Contents

Foreword

Pope Francis declared 2025 as a Holy Year of Jubilee for the Catholic Church, an event that normally takes place every twenty-five years. The theme for the Jubilee is 'Pilgrims of Hope'. The Jubilee arrives at a time when there is so much suffering in our world as a result of war, poverty, division, uncertainty and climate change.

The Pilgrims of Hope Jubilee presents each one of us with an opportunity to reignite the flame of hope in our hearts and to share the light of that hope with those experiencing darkness. Hope is something deeper than optimism. The late Rabbi Jonathan Sacks, in his book *To Heal a Fractured World: The Ethics of Responsibility,* teaches that 'optimism is the belief that the world is changing for the better; hope is the belief that, together, we can make the world better'.

In the following pages of *Dipping into Hope*, Fr Alan explores the meaning of hope and how it can touch the reality of our lives. He reminds us that we are on this journey together, and, despite the many real challenges, if we open our hearts to hope then great possibilities await us! These reflections are born out of Fr Alan's vast experience of life and ministry. He has seen how hope can bring encouragement and strength to those who journey in dark places. This book of reflections offers us the chance to find hope in the 'bits and pieces' of everyday life, as Patrick Kavanagh put it.

Since coming to Dublin earlier this year, I have had the opportunity of getting to know Fr Alan in his life and ministry. What strikes me about Alan is his great gift to see the deeper meaning in what we might describe as the 'ordinary'. Put another way, he possesses the great gift of imagination, which is needed now more than ever. This gift enables us to reflect upon our reality and opens us up to what is possible. St John Henry Newman reminded us that 'the heart is commonly reached not through reason but through the imagination'. In these reflections Alan is reaching out to our hearts and is inviting us to look at the world imaginatively, through the prism of hope. This is only possible for someone who has walked the road of life and has immersed themselves in the drama and mystery it entails. In my experience of knowing Alan, his relationship with the person of Jesus is the foundation for all that he does. In his encounter with others, he sees the mystery and the hope that is Christ. I am deeply grateful that he has shared these reflections in *Dipping into Hope* to help us strengthen our own relationship with Christ and to experience his hope-filled presence in new ways.

In his introduction to the Papal Bull *Spes non Confundit,* Pope Francis writes that 'in the heart of each person, hope dwells as the desire and expectation of good things to come, despite our not knowing what the future will bring'. As disciples of Jesus, we know that in him, our ultimate hope, good things will come! The Year of Jubilee has begun, and the Holy Door in St Peter's Basilica has been opened by the Pope. May the following reflections in *Dipping into Hope* encourage us to be pilgrims of hope as we cross the threshold into this special year.

With prayerful good wishes,
†Paul Dempsey,
Auxiliary Bishop of Dublin

Introduction

Settling back into the city of Dublin following a time away had its challenges. It was the first time I ever came back to the city without having the comfort of a family home. In the past, mam and dad were always there to drop in on; I could share a meal with them, meet neighbours or grab a night's sleep. But they died, and the family home had to be sold.

Apart from this adjustment, I was also asked to take up an appointment in the parish of City Quay in Dublin's Docklands. When I eventually settled, a lot of my day was spent walking up and down the quays. I noted that many were dealing in and taking drugs. It's a sad sight to see many young people suffering the pain and torment of addiction and yet compulsively seeking out that which destroys them. I remembering thinking if 'dope' (colloquial word for drugs in Dublin) can be found on the quay, why can't hope be found too?

Looking at the small church, in need of repair, that opens onto the River Liffey, I saw many good people working hard to keep the church open so locals and visitors could enter, pray and reflect. Despite all the developments on Dublin's docks, there are very few buildings, if any, that one can enter without making a purchase or having a security pass. As a matter of fact, on Sir John Rogerson's Quay and City Quay the church may be only building that people are free to enter and leave without any obligation other than to preserve the atmosphere of prayer and reflection. In a small way this gives hope to many.

I was in the midst of these reflections when I heard that Pope

Francis had declared 2025 as a Jubilee Year of Hope. Furthermore he wrote an inspiring document, *Spes non Confundit* (*SC*), telling us that 'hope does not disappoint' (Rom 5:5). In the first paragraph he tells us that 'in the heart of each person, hope dwells as the desire and expectation of good things to come'. Never was there a more opportune time to contemplate the importance of hope. In his letter to the Corinthians, St Paul says of love, faith and hope that 'the greatest of these is love' (1 Cor 13:13). This was Paul's view, but the community of the early Church were in no doubt, following on from the experience of the resurrection, that the greatest of these was hope. Jesus chiselled his way into our existence to bring us hope where we thought there was none, namely beyond sickness, death and the grave.

This short book of reflections, in the spirit of this Jubilee year, aims to show you that hope is not a distant reality. What we hope for is in the here and now – in our present reality. Those who are members of the Church are asked to minister hope in our 'now'. The now of many is difficult today. Even our concern for the environment makes many young people feel that there is no hope, as we plunder and manipulate creation. Alongside other issues like the threats and realities of war, growing homelessness, the unaffordability of housing and increasing problems with mental health, there was never a better time to be bearers and bringers of hope. Though many of these reflections may not include the word 'hope', it is my hope that you will find hope among them both explicitly and implicitly.

By far the most significant reason to sit down, ponder, write and edit material for another book is the encouraging conversations you have with people based on your last book. I am in no doubt that this is the reason why I put pen to paper on this publication entitled *Dipping into Hope*. The single most discussed item from my last publication was a short reflection on swimming.

I raised the issue of my fear of the water and how it inhibited my ability to enjoy the ocean. Happily I have overcome that fear, largely irrational, but very real when I had it. While fear may get in the way of swimming, it appears that it can also get in the way of the deeper issues.

I'm glad I'm not afraid of the ocean anymore. I am also glad that I am not afraid of things beyond and of the search for hope, as they are probably the most inspiring, generative and embracing aspects of living that I have ever encountered, and I wish to engage with them even more. I do this with the aid of prayer, reading, conversation, forgiveness and what is called the sacramental life. These things are both nourishment for the journey and much-needed signposts on the road of life. I find, though, that the greatest support to me is the person of Jesus, whose life and death have helped me lose my fear of transcendental matters. He also struggled to share, understand and live with the limitations of humanity. Everywhere he went he brought hope – in all that was imaginable and even in the unimaginable – and he continues to do this each and every day.

I hope and pray that these short reflections take away your fear and help you embrace possibility. Maybe this book will help you get in over your ankles or even to dive beneath the waves of mystery, where you can discover anew or rediscover the virtue of real and lasting hope in the present moment. Pope Francis asks that Christians become pilgrims of hope in this Jubilee year. This book is designed in such a way that you can carry it with you on your daily journey, taking time to dip in and out of it to find a thought or a refection that may inspire you to dive more deeply into the mystery we call God.

The purpose of hope is not to please God but to allow us to flourish and to share that flourishing with others. God not only wants us to be as fully alive as possible, but he needs us to be alive so that he can rejoice in us and see his very self reflected more fully in us.

'All of us need to recover the joy of living, since men and women, created in the image and likeness of God, cannot rest content with getting along one day at a time, settling for the here and now and seeking fulfilment in material realities alone' (*SC*, 9).

#Anger

Spending a week with a First Nation chief in Canada is no ordinary experience. I have many rich memories of my visit, as he is a very wise man and also very humorous. His insights into life, food, nature, medicine, respect, forgiveness and culture were astounding.

One of the most interesting thoughts he shared with me was that his people had no word for punishment. I looked at him, puzzled, and he went on to explain that if anyone, even a child, was angry and upset, they'd be sent to the anger pole in the tepee and asked to remain there until their anger passed. If they were a bit older, they might be told to head off in their canoe and wrestle with their spirit and return when their anger was no more. In other words, rather than being punished for their behaviour, they were asked to take time to ponder why it was there, work it out and then let it go.

This would prove too frightening for many in our culture today, who can live with anger as a default position. It can be easier to dump your troubles on someone else and stay angry. Exploring your anger and taking some responsibility can sometimes be too much. There are many things happening in our world to be angry about, but our anger should be prompting us to act rather than keeping us stuck and going around in destructive circles.

The chief told me some of the things he could have been angry about in his life, and there were a lot, but the anger would have destroyed him and those he loved. In his teaching he said that you cannot understand everything, so you have to let things go or they drag you down. Interestingly, even at this stage of his life, he still sits in his canoe!

We can all carry unnecessary burdens, stuff that we'll never understand. Pondering, praying and mediating are not necessarily narcissistic, passive acts. They can assist us to move on to better, freer ways of being. We may not have a tepee or a canoe, but we can cultivate spaces where we listen deeply and let go of things. It can be a rock, a mountain, a church or just a favourite place in the garden – somewhere we can unshackle ourselves from unnecessary nonsense, including anger.

Dublin's 40 foot

#Balance

I'm sure it has happened to you on several occasions. You carry your coffee to your table, sit down while placing it carefully, pull in to enjoy it and bump! – the table rocks and your drink ends up all over the place. It's the most annoying thing. You might be lucky if an observant employee spots your distress and gets you another drink 'on the house'. Failing this, you make your way back to the counter and start all over again.

As a result, I avoid sitting on stools or at high tables because, inevitably, they rock. If I must, I find a few beer mats or napkins and work out which is the short leg and plug the gap with them. I've noticed that three-legged tables seldom rock about like four-legged ones do. Whatever it is about the balance, I trust the three-legged ones more.

Getting the perfect balance is hard work. Oh, if only it was as easy in life to stuff a beer mat into whatever bits of our lives are out of sync. We say that we want to restore balance to our life as if it can be achieved in the blink of an eye. Balance is an ideal and ideals are hard to achieve.

For me, the path towards balance is ensuring that I know how many legs there are. The single most important leg for me, and the one that helps me to restore balance to my life, is the spiritual one. Somehow, it can compensate and assist the weaknesses of the other ones, and it gives me an energy to work with whatever is rocking about in my life.

Today it is common enough to deny the spiritual self and to dwell only on all that is rational or sensational. Karl Jung likened religious impulse to an instinct, and 'like every instinct, it has its specific energy, which it does not lose even if the conscious mind ignores it'.

So, if your life is a bit rocky and you are trying to get the balance right – make sure you check all your legs.

Sailing off the coast of Maine in the US

#Begin!

During our summers, when I hear the dawn chorus and feel the heat of the sun's rays piercing through the curtains of my bedroom, the words of the late Brendan Kennelly's poem occasionally come to my waking mind.

Begin again to the summoning birds
to the sight of the light at the window.

These days stir a lot of memories, as I think of summer encounters, visits and journeys. I would often meet Brendan on Parnell Street, while he was on his walk around Dublin. Most times he'd be wearing his long raincoat or a smart sports jacket, depending on the day's weather. His head would most often be uncovered, bringing attention to his wavy curls and his endearing smile. We'd often chat about things; he loved a bit of uncomplicated banter.

The literary agent Richard Pine tells us that Brendan once described poetry as 'something written by blind people groping for the light'. In this sense, then, most of us are poets, as we seek light, even enlightenment, on this hallowed journey we refer to quite simply as 'life'.

However, darkness can descend on us personally in moments of despair or anxiety. It too can envelop us socially as institutions collapse, leaving us fraught and frightened. Darkness can also enshroud us when a country is plunged into war or famine.

Brendan tells us that if we wish to be poets, this is not achieved by being mere passive recipients in adverse situations – we can reach for the light. This involves getting up, moving, thinking, reflecting, searching, even seizing – otherwise we risk remaining victims of circumstances often not of our own creation. Indeed, summer tells us that even the darkest night holds a hint of the dawn.

I marvel at how Brendan found words. Whether they came at him forwards, backwards, sideways or even edgeways, they are filled with hope and destiny. They are the gift of a blind man bringing light to our darkness. Many of his words encourage us to sit up and begin again – even in those moments when we don't feel we can.

Timber in a wood shed run by the Amish community in Indiana

#Break-up

It took a while, but over the course of a few conversations they realised that the relationship had to end. It was a very difficult conclusion, as they had put months, even years of effort into creating this bond. There were endless hours spent looking at a mirror, tossing hair from side to side, shaping it with various gels, consultations with hair stylists, finding the right clothes to accentuate their best selves, and there were countless photographs taken and deleted until finally what were thought to be the 'coolest' were shared.

This 'other' with whom they shared their life initially brought a buzz of excitement and energy into their world. They felt good in their presence, uplifted, even needed and wanted. Then something went wrong. It got to be hard work, and the effort didn't bring the results they expected.

Some break-ups can be done by text. Others can't. They require more heartfelt engagement. And then, you wonder, are you doing the right thing? What if you discover that you've made an awful mistake?

But the decision was made and acted on. And this other person? Not actually another person but rather an online profile that they had created of themselves. It was the person they thought they should be rather than who they were. The comments, thoughts and pictures posted were less and less about who they really were and how they really felt, and more and more about how they wanted or needed to be perceived by others. Over time it all become very hollow, and they found themselves living a life they couldn't understand. The initial excitement and energy gave way to strange, empty feelings, so the relationship ended.

It was obvious that a break was necessary. They needed to spend more time with the person that they were and less time with the person that they thought they should be – shutting down their cyber-self gave them the space to be in better company.

It's hard to be two people at one and the same time – it is infinitely more pleasurable to discover the unique and phenomenal person that you truly are. St John Henry Newman advised us 'to act on what we have, since we have not what we wish'.

A site being developed on Dublin's quay-side

Capitalism

I remember my first experience with capitalism. Let me give a little background first. Every summer many Dublin families packed up and left suburban dwellings to venture to their extended families around the country or to the numerous seaside resorts around the coast of Ireland.

For us it was Skerries most of the time – it was still within the county of Dublin, but in our childhood minds it was far, far away. We packed the car and travelled to this seaside resort, and we were sentenced to two weeks in a caravan. I am in no doubt that if I were a musician, I'd have composed a few 'rhythm and blues' tunes to the sound of the raindrops on the caravan roof where I pined away the hours looking for a break in the clouds.

The years that were different and exciting were the years that I took up fishing. It took me a while to get used to rod, reel, weight, float, hook and bait, to say nothing of the knots. In economic terms these were the 'factors of production' that facilitated my entrepreneurial spirit. It took a while, but eventually I got it right and I caught my first mackerel, then my second, then my third and so on. I quickly discovered there are only so many mackerel that one can cook and eat! Furthermore, the fact that the fish were cooked on an open pan in a caravan meant that the fumes filled the air – you went to sleep to the smell of fried mackerel, and you woke up to the same odour!

Then, as I said, I discovered capitalism. As I caught more and more fish, people standing around on the pier wanted to buy them. I charged ten pence for each one and discovered financial independence from my parents and the excitement of having my own money to spend at the amusements that night. My father taught me the most important lesson that I ever learned about the free market and capitalism – the money I earned wasn't solely for me. It was beholden on me to share it with my family. Every evening, before we went out to the amusements, we shared the pot. Oh, what fun we had. These ideas always come to mind when I read the gospel of Jesus in John 21:6, which encouraged the disciples to cast their net out to the other side. It took a while to get the technique right before I drew in the few mackerel on the fishing line, but once it happened, I began to be oblivious to the rain and enjoyed my profiteering. Whenever I read that gospel, I can sense the excitement of those in the boat who benefited from the Lord's kindly intervention.

Chicago reflected in 'The Bean'

#Chief O'Neill

The O'Neill Collection of Traditional Irish Music is one of the great treasures in the library of the University of Notre Dame in Indiana. Born in 1848, Francis O'Neill arrived in Chicago in 1870. He started working on the shoreline and then joined the police force, ending up as chief of police.

O'Neill hailed from County Cork, and he had a great love of Irish music, as evidenced by his flute playing. When he settled in the US, he was genuinely afraid that Irish music would disappear due to the impact of famine and emigration. Rather than sitting back and deploring the situation, he set about collecting tunes, eventually publishing the largest volume of Irish traditional music ever collected – 1,850 melodies.

Most Irish music is learned by ear and repetition. Writing the tune down in collections was a novel way of remembering. Stories are told of the chief collecting music from the many people he met. One of his greatest sources were the cells in Chicago's jails. If he heard of an Irishman in the lock-up, he'd visit and, after some initial introductions, he'd ask if they had any tunes. Sure enough they'd share a few bars, explaining the name, origin and context of the tune. There was many a man who lilted his way out of the clink!

During my time in the University of Notre Dame, I had the honour of viewing the O'Neill collection. Seeing the detail, the beautiful handwriting and the variety of sources was indeed inspiring. O'Neill's own notations in pencil were on books that were passed on to him. He shared the English and Irish names of the various tunes, whether they were reels, hornpipes or polkas, and, more importantly, who wrote them.

No doubt he had a passion for Irish music and his Irish heritage. What I've learnt from O'Neill is that passion is more than a feeling. The true evidence of passion is a decision. We often hear conversations about what people are passionate about, and it stays at the bar or at the dining table. As I browsed the extraordinary books in the library, I wondered what decisions the chief, were he alive today, would be taking about the things that we need to preserve.

My favourite session in The Cobblestone Pub in Dublin

Christmas Soup

The soup was simmering nicely. Just a final check to make sure the flavour was right. It was made out of a lovely array of vegetables cooked in a very good chicken stock. I reached for the spoon to conduct a final taste test. More seasoning was required. Salt levels were okay, but a bit of black pepper was needed. When the soup is for Christmas dinner, one must go the extra mile.

I reached up to the cupboard above me and caught hold of the small jar with the peppercorns. Turning it upside down, I twisted the lid that grinds the peppercorns into smaller grains of black pepper. Whoops! The peppercorns just slid out of the jar into the soup. I hurriedly put the jar down, reaching for an implement that would help me rescue the peppercorns and, indeed, the soup. However, I noticed that the peppercorns looked a tad clumsy, and it was only when I started fishing them out that I realised that I'd added a jar of cloves to the mix. Try as I might, I could not collect anywhere near the number of cloves that had been in the jar before I emptied its contents. I tasted the soup again in the hope that maybe they wouldn't be noticed. It was just awful – I'm sure if I'd had a Geiger counter to hand I'd have come up with a positive reading!

I discovered that day that no matter how good the chef or cook is, if the ingredients aren't right then the food won't be right. The same is true of life and of the season that we celebrate. Christmas has become many things, so much so that it has even lost its name, and this great feast is now commonly referred to as a 'winter break'. Regardless of this dominant narrative, the main ingredient of the season for me is the realisation best expressed by Athanasius, the fourth-century mystic, who said that 'God become one of us so that we too could become like God'. This truth came to mind when listening to Bono on Brendan O'Connor a few weeks ago. He didn't mention cloves, but he did say something about the ingredients of his faith when he said that 'love in the abstract can become concrete, and it can change lives, but love to me is best expressed in a child born in dung and straw'.

Night time on Dublin's quays with Samuel Beckett Bridge swinging open

#Civilisation

There is a lot wrong with Christianity, and there is a lot wrong with Catholicism. Given all that is reported about their limitations, institutions have the uncanny knack of obscuring or overlooking what is good about them.

I grew up in a rough-and-tumble Church. It wasn't perfect. Every Sunday I came across people who left me wondering if they had the right to be present at Mass, primarily because I didn't like them. The reason may have been as important as having chased us away when we played football on the green outside their house. I met priests who were far from perfect, but somehow, despite all their faults, they did their best, and they were loved. In a suburban world where there was the risk of nothingness, the parish was a generous centre that provided opportunities for human relationships, gatherings, grief and fun. It looks like much of this is changing utterly or may even disappear.

This is the nature of things. Religious faith, regardless of its denomination, always subsists in a culture or civilisation. Sometimes it wields power and influence in that culture, at other times it is disregarded or even ostracised. However, since the times of the Greeks and the Romans there have been constant discussions and shades of agreement about the role of the divine presence and its institutional expression in the world. Aristotle wrote in his *Metaphysics*, 'there is something that moved without being moved – something which is eternal'. The Romans believed that the emperor was God, and the emperors then came to believe that they were 'god-like', which was often the beginning of their downfall. No matter how empty the pews are, Western civilisation remains moored to its Greco-Judaeo-Christian origins. The philosopher Jürgen Habermas, who professes no particular faith, tells us that much of what we know today and which holds us together as a society and as democracy is as a direct result of the Jewish concept of mercy and the Christian ethic of love.

The granite steps descending into the River Liffey in Dublin

#Classroom

I was intrigued by the painting by the South Korean artist Dong Wook Suh entitled *Summer Morning*. I have begun to call this work 'The Covid Classroom', since it depicts life during the pandemic. A young person lies on a bed, the sunbeams hitting at an angle across the room. The sunlight that is trying to nurture the young person's soul is avoided. On the bed there is an open laptop, and on the wall a socket is laden with various chargers. On a nearby table there is a mobile phone, along with an open cigarette packet and a lighter.

This is a far cry from the idea of a classroom that comes to our minds. A lecture room in a modern university can seat anything from 20 to 400 people, or even more. Sometimes we know those around us, at other times we are shy among strangers, but we passively await opportunities to get to know them.

I noticed that when we were told we could return to college post-Covid, it wasn't negotiated very well. It was presumed that we could just slot back into someone else's idea of what was right and appropriate. Maybe we had got used to the classroom depicted in Dong Wook Suh's painting. It was something we could switch on and off, whether we were in bed or in our part-time jobs, and remain partially engaged.

At the university in which I was chaplain, I began to realise that a university is not just a place for academic opportunities, but it is a space to grow, flourish and engage as people, especially in undergraduate courses. Wharton psychologist Adam Grant has created a new post-Covid category: 'the middle child of well-being'. It lies between flourishing and depression, and it is called languishing; the more colloquial expression is CBB – couldn't be bothered.

Maybe the subject in Dong Wook Suh's painting knows that middle child. The only way out of languishing, the experts say, is to act your way out of it; thinking about moving on doesn't really help. It only leaves us languishing for longer. So, whatever your pursuit, don't just languish – live!

The show jumping arena in the RDS Dublin

Contentment

'We are born with a bucket, or some such container, and we spend the first half of life filling it up with things and the second half of life emptying it of those same things.' I remember hearing these words from the writer and retreat-giver Richard Rohr. They crossed my mind the other day when I sat with my ninety-two-year-old aunt in her room at her nursing home. I always looked forward to our visits – they gave me great life, though her memory was fading, her eyesight greatly weakened and her hearing was far from what it was. However, looking at her few belongings in the room, I realised that she has emptied her bucket of quite a lot. The one thing that remained with her though is a great deal of contentment. Our conversations always end with her saying, 'Thank God for so much'.

I don't know what phase of life you are at: maybe that phase where you are preoccupied with filling your bucket full of stuff that you need, think you need or others think you need; maybe you are trying to empty the bucket of what is unnecessary, burdensome or downright useless; maybe you should be emptying your bucket, but you continue to fill it with ridiculous things. I think I am realising more and more the need to empty mine.

The spiritual journey is essentially a journey of letting go. There are days and rituals in liturgy for saying goodbye to someone and literally waiting for 'God knows what!' I find that I often lack the courage and wisdom to know what to say goodbye to. My instincts are to hold on to everything for no reason other than that they are familiar and comforting. Rohr tells us that authentic spirituality is really letting go of things. To let go of a lot of things that we thought we couldn't live without is, most often, a liberation. I hope and pray that when I let go of things, I find that somewhere in my rusty bucket is that wonderous gift of God, namely the contentment that my Aunt Kitty radiates.

Candles burn at the grotto in the University of Notre Dame

#Death

'Death is very final, child.' This was one of my mother's sayings. The words are few, but they are laden with truth. Her own mother died when mam was sixteen, and it was obvious that she never really got over it – thus the heavy weight with which she carried and uttered these words.

They rang through my entire being when she died. As I gazed upon her serene, lifeless face, those words – 'Death is very final, child' – shook me.

Remembering the dead is far from a morbid exercise. Anniversaries, birthdays and days like All Souls' Day are times to remember those who have died, those we have known and miss – and maybe it is also a day to feel the rawness of death's finality. But it is also an opportunity to stop doing and thinking and to spend some time pondering. Taking time to stand on the edge of life as we understand it is adventurous. Do we peer into nothingness or investigate something that can only be described as 'beyond'?

Though I am a Catholic, and a priest, I often have to wander outside my heavily secularised and Westernised religious affiliation to enhance the time I spend pondering. Time spent with indigenous peoples reminds me that the concepts of beginning and end are very much a Western worldview. Unlike the privatised spirituality of the West, indigenous cultures believe that spirit is the core thread that binds individuals together into communities. They also believe that we are part of the community that lies beyond the limitations of the human categories of time and space. We are one – there is no 'other'; there is only us.

Psalm 41 speaks of 'deep calling unto deep', which is not unlike that deep listening referred to as *dadirri* among indigenous peoples of Australia. *Dadirri* runs deep – it is a quietness and a listening that fosters a state of connection with all that exists. The closest translation of this word is contemplation.

Miriam-Rose Ungunmerr Baumann of the Ngangikurungkurr (Nan-ge-cur-ung-cur) tribe explains this form of living in the following way:

'There are deep springs within each one of us. Within this deep spring, which is the very Spirit of God, there is a sound. The sound of Deep calling to Deep. The sound is the Word of God – Jesus.'

So, Miriam Rose and mam, I pray for the grace to listen and to listen deeply to discover the sound of the great spring that is common to us all, and so move beyond limited thinking and limited living.

#Epiphany

In every sense of the word, they came late to the gig. If the wise men were travelling to the equivalent of a party, they'd be arriving when the chairs were being stacked, the tables were being moved away, the floors were being swept and the band were loading their gear into the van.

They are often referred to as Magi, which comes from the Persian word *Magush*. Having their origins in Zoroastrianism, they were known for their scholarly achievements and were skilled astrologers and astronomers. Their dress and their gifts tell of people from a different place. In fact, the tone of their skin in visual representations hints at the three known continents in the world at that point in time, namely Africa, Asia and Europe. They also represent the three ages of humanity – youth, middle age and those who are older. All these elements suggest that this was a global event of universal significance.

It wasn't easy for the three, who encountered in the cunning and scheming of Herod the epitome of narrow-mindedness, insecurity and deviousness. Herod had power, learning and authority, but these traits don't guarantee wisdom. He tried to lure the three into his web of intrigue, but wisdom helped them find another way, and they travelled a different road.

We know only too well that wisdom is not the possession of men, nor of those of rank, nor is it granted in academic degrees. Wisdom can be found among the most humble and ordinary of people. Indeed, Scripture reveals numerous wise women who helped keep the plan of God grounded in people's reality. Ruth, Naomi and Sarah are great examples of this.

Every day we too can be sucked into narrow roads that lead to doom and despair – but wisdom can teach us other ways to maintain integrity and give hope. With the flush and energy of youth, we can often rush headlong into sticky situations, but even when wisdom arrives late it is welcome, just like the Magi. It is first and foremost a gift that we seek while creating the disposition for it. We know that the greatest barrier to wisdom is the ego, as exemplified in the person of Herod. I am reminded of a time when someone asked why wise people are important. The reply was precisely because they don't need to be.

Looking towards the Poolbeg Lighthouse from 'The Half Moon'

Evil

There are some words that I don't like to hear. One of those words is 'evil'. These days, with so many innocent people dying needlessly because of immoral and illegal acts, it's very hard not to think of the word 'evil'. The Russian writer Maria Stepanova expressed it another way when she said, 'We exist and act in the black hole of another's consciousness.'

Evil is a concept that I considered in philosophical and theological studies many years ago. However, it was never as real to me as when I met a woman who lived through the Rwandan genocide. She described the moment when a gun was put to her head by a member of the militia for the third time over the same number of weeks. She hoped and prayed that she'd be shot as she was tired of waiting to be killed – she just wanted it over.

In our conversation I couldn't ignore the intensity of the evil that seemed to be at the heart of all the murdering and depravity. I needed to know how she dealt with it when it was happening and how she managed it in her memory. 'Do you believe in evil?' I asked her. 'When you see it, smell it and taste it – you cannot but believe it exists,' she replied, and then she looked straight at me and said, 'but once you see it, you have no choice but to turn around and spend the rest of your life walking towards all that is good – there is no choice in this – there is no other option.' 'What does that mean?' I asked. Calmly she answered, 'I now spend my life placing goodness on the throne of God. When I see goodness – and there is a lot of it – I just put it back at God's feet and thank him for it.'

She often comes to mind when I hear of various atrocities across the world. We need not live in another's dark consciousness. Let us not lose sight of goodness, and let us hope and pray that goodness will dissolve some, if not all the evil, which can sometimes appear to be the most dominant force at play.

Down at the Poolbeg lighthouse
on Dublin's South Wall

Freedom

Saturday nights involved rituals. Shoes were polished and left at the front door. Baths were run, fresh clothes were laid out and treats were the order of the night. All this effort was to prepare for a day that rocked to a different rhythm. There was always a plan to discuss for the next day, usually involving a visit to relatives and meeting with some of the numerous cousins scattered around Dublin. The favourite trip though was always to Wicklow, where us city dwellers learned that there were other and more satisfying ways to live. As Sunday evening crept up on us, the impending heaviness of Monday morning and school cast its shadow over the fun and adventure; we dragged ourselves back into the city-bound car.

They were great days. Shops were for the large part closed, even petrol stations closed early, and quite often we got home on the smell of the petrol in the tank. Sunday was when new clothes were worn, but there was always a bag somewhere in the car with 'the change of clothes', allowing us to scramble up and down mountains and over fences and walls. And for the visiting Dub – collecting the eggs was both *egg*sciting and fascinating – a realisation that life wasn't always about shops, cartons and bottles.

I remember it as a lighter day, brimming over with adventure and freedom. I believe this happened for the large part because it was a Sunday – a day of religious observance – or Sabbath, as it is also known. Most religions have a day of the week with a different rhythm that demands a little bit extra or even a little bit less. I've heard many definitions of this day since my childhood, and I've experienced it in many manifestations. My favourite understanding of the Sabbath is based on a piece I read recalling the escape of the Jewish people from Egypt. The Sabbath was established not primarily for religious observance, in a narrow sense, but as a day to celebrate the fact that I am no longer a slave. When I have a day off or I'm on holiday, I often look to the heavens and say I'm nobody's slave today. Try it someday soon and give these days of slick entrapment the flick.

Looking east on Dublin's quays

#Geese

Nature can be one of our finest teachers, if we'd care to listen. Every year I spot the arrival of the Brent geese. Having flown more than four thousand miles from Canada, stopping off at Iceland along the way, they spend their winter in places that are easier to live in.

Geese have an incredible moral and physical compass, which assists them on their journey from Canada. For instance, their 'V' formation allows for shared leadership and energy conservation – the one out front will drop back, allowing others to take the lead. Their constant honking reminds the leaders that they haven't lost those who follow behind.

Scholarship reveals that when creatures like geese migrate they don't adopt the casual Irish attitude of 'Ah, sure lads, we'll see how it goes.' They stick to a direct flight path, without veering left or right for the goose equivalent of a quick pint, a party or having the craic! Any stop on the route is purposely designed to further the journey's progress. Detours, if they are made, are taken if the weather takes a turn for the worse.

Recently I was reading a book about leadership by Hubert Joly. He is particularly skilled at bringing businesses back from the edge of extinction and collapse. Reflecting on his most successful ventures, he identifies two essential ingredients of leadership. Ironically these appear to be in the genetic code of geese. The elements are purpose and connection.

There is no doubt that life can be difficult if we have lost our purpose. I recall the words of a wise man who once upon a time encouraged us to 'look at the birds of the air'. If we find it difficult to take direction from the wisdom of our Christian traditions, perhaps we can look to the geese for similar inspiration.

Sunset off the coast of Maine

#Glendalough

Over the years I've taken many people to Glendalough. My favourite groups are the international students from various countries and from a range of faith backgrounds. A general theme is to discuss how this rich past informs our present. The beauty of the place provides an experience in itself and one always hopes for kindly weather to enhance it.

From a tourist's point of view, the main attraction is the lakes and the monastic ruins. However, I can never start there. I always make my way to the upper lake and work back towards the monastery. There is a method in my madness. I sit the students at the lakeside across from St Kevin's Bed, the cave where Kevin set up home in the sixth century. After some silence, while taking in birdsong and the lapping of the water on the shore, I ask them to ponder why Kevin came here in the first place. The obvious answer that many give is to find God. I wonder if that's a bit presumptuous!

Our own experience of 'finding God' is not like going to a shop and ordering something. We often find God when we are looking for something else. More often, God comes to us at a time we least expect or even want. So why did Kevin come to this valley in Wicklow? Was he escaping or running away, or was he just plain frustrated with whatever he left behind? Frustration is a common theme that runs across the centuries.

Was he frustrated with his family and their expectations of

him, or the subliminal messages put his way by those who were trying to shape and influence him? Was it the politics and leadership of the day? Kevin didn't come to Glendalough to build a monastic village, but it happened because his inward journey created an outward expression. Maybe it was his frustrations that were the foundation of it all. The ensuing conversations with the students about their frustrations with life as we journey onwards are always amazing. Following Kevin's inspiration, perhaps the things about which we are frustrated now contain the seeds of a great future.

A flower in the Burren, County Clare

#Hacked

'I've been hacked.' What an aggressive phrase. Hacking is an aggressive act, as it involves tearing something apart and putting it back together again. Something that had a form and purpose is torn apart and reassembled for some end other than that for which it was intended.

We've all seen a movie in which some sinister character is trying to destroy the world or a good character is trying to save it, and they 'hack' into a computer mainframe to undo a program or change its intended purpose. This may make a great premise for a movie, but most hacking is done by other computers, not individuals – hundreds of machines targeting one system until it is cracked and manipulated.

Maybe it's easy to sit back and imagine all these machines working against or with one another to achieve a sinister purpose. Whatever about machines, there is no doubt that our minds can be 'hacked' too. How many things in any one moment during our day are trying to hack us? Maybe the purpose isn't all that sinister, but increasingly our minds, hearts and souls are surrendering their will to an infinite number of subtle hacks as bright lights and pings try to seduce us away from whatever noble or necessary task or purpose we were initially focused on.

Funnily enough, prayer has a profound purpose other than seeking things that we want from God. It is a way of recentring and reclaiming our lives in the event of a mental hack. I continue to be greatly inspired by the moments when Jesus escaped to the desert or went off in a boat on his own. There was no internet in Palestine in his day, but there were those annoying distractions, voices that tried to lure him away from the purpose or tasks that gave him life and peace. It was in these moments, while taking refuge in the desert or in boats, that he went away to reclaim his soul and avoid the babble of the hackers who tried to reassemble him into their own image and purpose. Simply put, when he was away on his own, he reclaimed his identity, he appeared to find peace and maybe he even got a chance to pray too!

Eden Quay, Dublin with
Liberty Hall stretching skywards

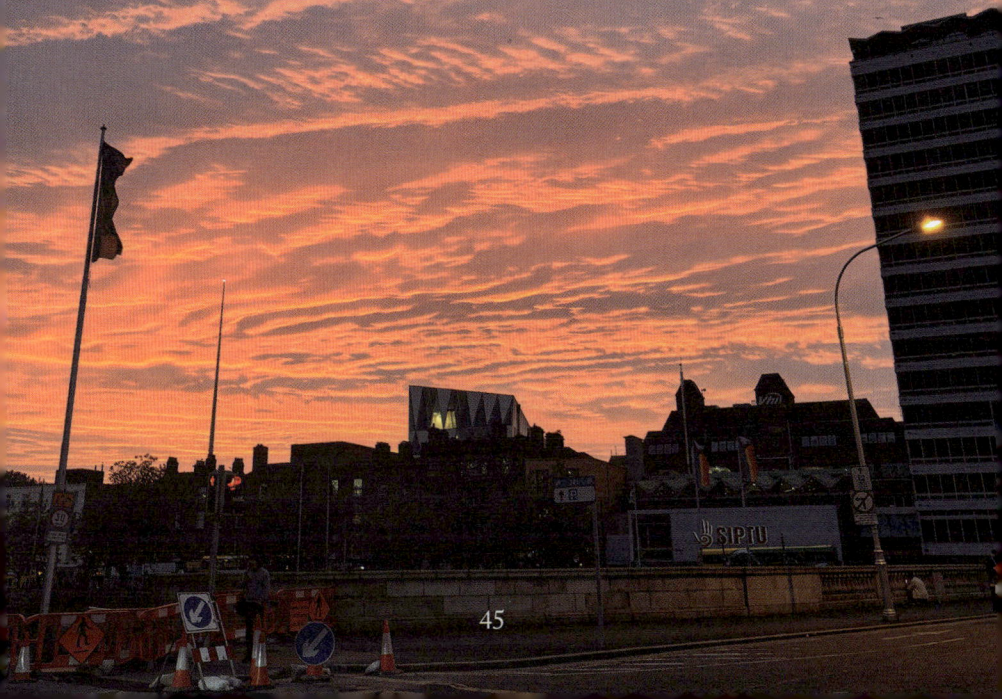

#Happiness

I was surrounded by happiness. It was coming at me from everywhere. I nearly had to run to avoid it. You see I was between those shelves in the bookshop that are labelled 'self-help', 'well-being' or some other such word that tries to capture esoteric states. As I stood there, happiness was bouncing off the shelves and knocking me about with the choice of guaranteed pathways to its doorstep.

There were humorous approaches to happiness, shortcuts to it, ten steps to the same goal. Some monks had the key; there were toolkits, too, and others who could get you to happiness in fifteen minutes. Some claimed to have captured the art of happiness and others could get you there with the aid of art. Another book said happiness was free – even though the book itself was quite expensive.

Being happy is important – how to get there can be a challenge. There are times in our year when we go crazy buying for ourselves and others. I've never yet seen an ad where someone out shopping or someone receiving a gift hadn't a smile on their face. It's as if every problem can be solved at the till or with a tap or a PIN number. Once upon a time all roads led to Rome – now they lead to the shops or the online store!

But getting back to happiness – someone once said to me, 'Happiness is not what you have – your happiness lies in what you wouldn't give away.' This short line has changed my idea of happiness. Now if it eludes me, I don't rush out to buy something. I think of all that I have that I wouldn't give away. When I do this, people come to mind, people I couldn't imagine my life without. I remember moments shared with people who are no longer with me but whose wisdom guides my feet every day. There are also places that give me peace and then there are other people who inspire me and who make me smile. And, of course, there is the continuous unfolding of my faith in God and God's faith in me, which brings me a happiness and joy that transcend any loyalty programme.

These roads or thoughts on happiness don't necessarily lead to Rome or the shops or even certain sections of bookshops, but in recalling these many blessings in my life, the things that I wouldn't give away, I find all the happiness I need.

A market in Quebec

#Inspire

The fabric of faith in Ireland has been shaped these last decades by the abuse of children and the perceived inaction of those in authority in both Church and state. A lot has been put in place, but when horrible things were happening there was little or nothing, only despair and isolation laden with pain.

My time as a priest has been overshadowed by abuse. Newly ordained a priest, I once shared a house with someone who had suffered a breakdown following a break-in and assault at his previous home. In my youthful enthusiasm, I went out of my way to ensure he felt safe. But I had been misled, his attacker was the father of a child he had abused; no one had told me.

As I think back, I know I went into shock, a shock that pales in comparison with the shock and pain of those abused and the psychological suffering of their families. There were times that I felt like packing it in, but the one thing that was akin to a pilot light of faith that kept me going was the victims and their families. They constantly amaze me. Over the years, despite being so badly hurt by the Church, they have held on to their faith in God. They remain in contact with me, greeting me always with kindness and warmth. If they can hold on to their faith, why can't I? I was asked to move from the parish soon after the reports of abuse surfaced. I chose to stay, politely refusing to move. I wondered if I moved would people think I was part of it all.

In those days no one wanted to talk about the real issues, and the isolation was blade-like in its impact, cutting deep into my soul. I'm sure many share this experience. I was briefed on what had happened by the local district nurse – no one from my diocese informed me. My mother spotted that all was not well, and we had a remarkable conversation in the front room of the family home when we concluded that the greatest threat to my faith was not secularism or doubt but the Church itself. Knowing the horror of all that was going on was a burden that was heavy to bear. Apart from two exceptional colleagues, fellow clergy didn't want to hear about it; slowly I was being perceived as the problem and even pathologised. When the *Murphy Report* on child abuse came out, one priest was kind enough to send a text saying, 'Alan, I never believed you about how bad it was.'

The victims with whom I have shared the journey remind me that Jesus didn't remain a victim – he got down from the cross and he was transformed. He wants to take us down from our crosses and transform our lives too. Often the agent of that transformation comes from the place you'd least expect.

Pottery sale in a small town outside Montreal

#Interconnected Loners

Walking through college one day, I came across a group of students who were stuck into their project. Their heads were down as they tried to get off to a good start.

College had just reopened after the Covid-19 pandemic, and we negotiated how best to catch up and check in on their mask-wearing world while observing social distancing.

'How are you coping with all the madness?' I asked. Thus began a conversation about life and how it is evolving in these strange times. I suppose it is a far cry from how they imagined college would be and, indeed, how their lives would be. In these simple conversations, though, is an opportunity to see where they are at, and, if nothing else, to help them be aware that they are not on their own in this 'madness'. Sometimes it happens this way – the word of another who shares a similar chaos or uncertainty provides a lifeline into a common humanity and a first step out of isolation.

They were genuinely trying to express how things were, so I lobbed in a high ball. 'I was reading a book during the week', I said. 'It's a conversation between a sociologist and a journalist, and they described how we are all being shaped by the goings-on in the world now, and one of their opinions was that we are becoming "interconnected loners". There was a definite pause, a light-bulb moment. 'That one hundred per cent it', one said, and another repeated the phrase as if he was tasting it.

Obviously, those words hit on something, and, if it was meaningful for them, it will surely open something for a lot of other people. 'Interconnected loners'. Yes, we can crow about the merits of the various platforms and how helpful they are, but they are no fun if we are switching them off only to be on our own. We only really grow in the company of others. As I think back to that short interaction with the students, I realise that the project was quite secondary to their engagement with one another. What they were doing was the antithesis of being an 'interconnected loner', and they were enjoying it. And that my friends is education: connection is life, 'one hundred per cent'.

Niagara Falls at night

#John Donne

At any hour of the day, we could quite easily be at one with the words of the poet John Donne. For instance, in his characteristically witty way, he speaks to the rising sun:

> *Busy old fool, unruly Sun,*
> *Why dost thou thus*
> *Through windows and through curtains, call on us.*

Donne's life spanned the late sixteenth and early seventeenth centuries. Ordained at the age of thirty-nine, he was the most popular preacher in London. When Charles I became king of England, Donne was commanded by him to preach at the coronation.

Maybe you waded through Donne's poems for various exams. You probably have navigated your way through 'Batter My Heart, Three Person'd God', 'The Good Morrow', 'Death Be Not Proud', and then 'When Thou Has Done, Thou Has Not Done, for I Have More'. Typical of Donne, he loads his need for God's energetic mercy with irony.

Life wasn't the easiest for him. His wife died at a very young age, and he lost two of his twelve children to various diseases that were rampant at the time. Following financial difficulties, he was flung into debtor's prison, which in those days was a room fourteen-and-a-half feet by twelve. The detainee had to pay for food or for the chance to have the locks on their chains removed or their prison door opened – this was how prisons were funded back then. Furthermore, at an existential level he found it hard to absorb Galileo's finding that the earth revolved around the sun. It shook him to the extent that he said, 'Tis all in pieces, all coherence gone'.

However, throughout his life and through all his difficulties, he had a deep sense of God. It was his life experiences that informed his preaching, and he made constant reference to his failures and how he overcame them. He also spoke in images from daily life, through which people were helped to connect with their faith. His core message can be summed up in his own words: 'It is astonishing to be alive and it behoves us to be astonished.' He never lost sight of the sheer loveliness of things or of people, saying, 'The human being is worth your awe, your attention and your love.' One great phrase of his was 'Tap a human ... and they ring with the sound of infinity.' So, before the 'unruly sun' sets today, give yourself a tap and hear infinity echo round about you.

Customs House, Dublin

#Kingfisher

I don't know about you, but summer keeps me awake. I don't mean that I am not sleeping, rather I am awake to so many things around me.

The long days aren't just about having more daylight hours – it's the way they create the possibility *to be more* and *to do more*. That's summer really, isn't it? It's sheer possibility, and it often starts with a simple moment that lies somewhere between beauty and mystery. It can be new growth or a magnificent sunset.

Last week while driving through the countryside, I pulled up beside a lake. Rather than jumping out of the car as I normally do, I sat sipping my coffee. I'm so glad I did, as I was about halfway down my cup when a bird landed on a reed nearby. I looked, and as this colourful bird turned its head towards me, I froze! For the first time in my life, a kingfisher and I shared the same space.

The flickering light on his body and pointed beak spoke of a searching, curious and industrious personality. At this stunning sight, everything instantly stopped for me. There was nowhere else I wanted to be, nor needed to be. This chance encounter was transformed into a moment of contemplation and privilege.

Wasn't it Gerard Manley Hopkins, an English poet and Jesuit priest, who spoke of kingfishers who catch fire? His complex yet beautiful poetic language simply tells us that we are all wonderful creatures in this magnificent creation. He goes on to tell us that to be happy and fulfilled we, like the kingfisher, just need to know how to do what we do best and to be who we are. To quote that poem: 'What I do is me, for that I came.' What an exquisite truth spoken in such an eloquent manner.

Life can get complicated and treacherous, especially when we want to be somebody that we are not or to be in some place other than where we are. This can be but a momentary thing or, sadly, for some, it can be a lifetime's preoccupation. While all this craziness is going on, it is nothing more than a distraction from all the glorious things that are happening all about us. Beauty and mystery are always dancing with one another, just as the light plays with the kingfisher's feathers. Oh, to be that kingfisher … to be as God's eye sees us. Nothing else matters.

'The Bean', Chicago

55

#Lament

A good traditional Irish music session can have you rocking and tapping with the rhythms that reverberate around the room. Tunes can be so contagious that dancers take to floor. However, a good session can also shift the emotional mood in moments when a musician shares what is known as a 'slow air'. Silence descends, other musicians fold up their instruments, bow their heads and breathe in the moment. Even if the session is in a pub, the glasses stop clinking. The few strangers, not accustomed to the ritual, are hushed, and they take the direction well.

A slow air often connects with a memory, a person or a moment that the musician wants to hold on to for ever. Some who sit alongside know that story well and so the respect and *anam chairdeachas* (soul connection) with both player and music are profound and religious. The tune may even acknowledge the unspoken sadness and brokenness of people's hearts in the present moment when the rage about difficult life situations lies beyond what words can express.

Laments are necessary. We could spend our lives trying to be rock 'n' roll kids or keep raving on, but there is a need to stop and capture moments of sadness. The Psalms are particularly good at this. Out of the 150 psalms, there are forty-two individual laments and sixteen expressing the lament of communities. A line from one is 'My soul is in anguish. How long, Lord, how long?'

Our human journey needs to name and be aware of the multitude of feelings and emotions that can take hold of our souls at any point in time. It may be easy to share the good ones and neglect the need to lament, but they only build up into something worse. Loss, grief and sadness are as real as joy, gratitude and happiness, but they may be more difficult to express. Thank God for the slow air and the Psalms, which allow us to capture these moments.

The Psalms also tell us we are not on our own in these difficult moments; furthermore, lament tells of a disoriented people calling out for a deeper and more wholesome reorientation of a life both here and in what lies beyond. Slow airs don't last for ever, and the session eventually finds its way back to the jigs, hornpipes and reels that can have us tapping once again.

Looking towards Dublin Port from the South Wall

#Leaders

'A fish rots from the head down.' The origin of this saying is unknown, but there is debate as to whether it is Greek, Turkish or Chinese. The basic thrust of the saying is that if there is a problem in an organisation then those that lead cannot be absolved of blame.

I've worked in many organisations throughout my life, and there is no doubt that the ethos of those in leadership makes its way into the heart and soul of the place. If leadership shows care, it is more likely that those who see and experience that care will respond in similar fashion. There are always exceptions, but emphasis on who we are and how we are to one another often bears more results than a constant hammering on what we do or what we are not doing.

I was recently involved, as a participant, in an organisational redesign that took no account of the values of the organisation, choosing to lose itself in politically correct jargon. I discussed this with a wise person who has successfully led many organisations throughout a long career, who said that redesign that doesn't start with values is a ship heading for the rocks.

It is more and more the case that interview processes based on competencies often neglect the basic social and interpersonal skills of those who are being promoted to positions of authority, thus creating organisations that lack warmth and purpose. A mantra of one of my great friends, a very successful salesperson and an inspiring leader, was 'people buy people'. If I like you and I trust you, there is more likelihood that I will buy whatever you are selling. The most important competency in leadership is often less about achievements on paper and more about how you manage those who journey with you and how they grow and develop in your presence. Sadly, it appears that less and less account is taken of these important aspects of leadership. After all, many of us can remember little of what we did when we held certain positions. Don't we more often remember the people we spent time with, some of whom have become great friends? If the fish has a healthy head the body will remain healthy too.

This photo was taken on the night of the Dublin riots. The irony of the situation was that Sina Theil was making a video to accompany her song 'Let There Be Peace' while the sirens wailed and smoke filled the air outside.

Leg Wax

He was from farming stock, she was a town girl. The banter between them told of a couple who got on well together and who understood one another – they laughed at the same things. One such occasion followed the birth of their first child. She spoke about the ordeal and mentioned that he was present at the birth and that he was of no use to her. He, with his usual droll, humorous take on things, said, 'Sure it was nothing new – I've seen a lot of lambings!'

The sparring had started. 'Well,' she said, '*if* and I mean if we are going to have another child, I'm going to make sure that you are strapped onto the table next to me, and as I am giving birth, you'll be getting your legs waxed!' Having neither given birth nor had my legs waxed, I can't say whether the two are worthy of comparison – I only know that he took a sharp intake of breath and the other people in our company cracked up with laughter. He had no reply!

When it came to the christening, I didn't know if I'd choose a reading about the 'pangs of childbirth' or the account of Samson getting his head shaved! There is always a biblical passage to suit the occasion. The Bible, especially the Old Testament, is full of the stoic reality that new things come with pain. Newness is seldom, if ever, cosy. There is the obvious groaning when there is physical movement and change, but there is also the inner turmoil of the bewildering loss of control that occurs as one steps into new spaces.

Referring to Psalm 77, where the distressed author feels that they have lost everything, even belief in God, the scripture scholar Martin Brueggemann says, 'As we seek to be faithful and as we seek to live in our culture [we] move from a religion of law to a religion of grace. It articulates the awareness that we live by gift and not by grasp.'

Thankfully, he doesn't mention the need to get my legs waxed!

The interactive sculpture called 'Pulse' on City Quay

#Nashville

When I arrived in Nashville, I tried to find the real country music sound. Years of listening to LPs and CDs had me primed for this moment. Nancy Griffith, Johnny Cash, The Highwaymen, Kris Kristofferson, Randy Travis, Loretta Lynn and the music from the epic movie *The Coalminer's Daughter* were among those sounds that had stuck in my soul and kept my feet moving down Broadway in Nashville. I was no sooner in two locations when I was met with versions of the Cranberries' 'In Your Head', which is an amazing song, but I didn't journey all the way to Tennessee to hear songs from the home country. Sharing my frustrations with some of the bartenders helped get a few good auld honky-tonk recommendations and, sure enough, before long I found country music heaven.

One place was right up my street. By day it sold boots and Stetsons, and by night its stage was occupied by various lead singers on guitar and others on double bass, dobro, banjo, harmonica and lyrical fiddle. There were drummers who could rattle out a rhythm sounding like a train car and, of course, a zinging pedal steel guitar that let out the necessary train whistle or wailing as required.

Driving through the hills of Kentucky and the coal mines of Tennessee is great preparation for Nashville. Clues as to the reason for the songs and their lyrics lie everywhere. Profound words from none other than Merle Haggard inscribed on the walls of the Country Music Hall of Fame tell us that 'country songs are the dreams of the working man'. A lump came to my throat and a tear to my eye when I read a note found on the body of a miner who suffocated following an Anderson County mine explosion in 1902: 'Goodbye Ellen, goodbye Lily, goodbye Jemmie. Is twenty-five minutes after two. There is few of us alive yet.'

Country music sings of God and Christianity as it sings of everything else of life in simple, ordinary and accessible words. Country musicians identify with a carpenter who knew and understood the fishermen, the farmers and those who travelled the roads. Most bands in the honky-tonk toasted the truck drivers who, they said, 'make sure our shelves are filled and our pantry has plenty'. It is a music that is in touch with life, but which doesn't try to dress it up as something its not.

#Nature

There are areas of the world that leave an indelible mark on your soul. Wyoming is one such place for me. In the words of Seamus Heaney, there are occasions that 'can catch the heart off guard and blow it open'. Invited by a friend of mine at the last minute with no clue where I was going, I set off only knowing that the state began with the letter 'W'.

Day and night, I walked on pristine packed snow in snowshoes, listening to the crunching beneath my feet while trying not to fall into drifts to the left and right of me. It was January, so much of the world of nature was hibernating.

Every day I encountered something different: elk, moose, foxes, wolves, bison (thankfully the bears were asleep in their caves). Bird life, too, was stunning, with woodpeckers, American bald eagles and grouse, and many other varieties. I met some park rangers who explained to me that bears move tons of soil to create their caves. The usually dig under trees, allowing the root structure to support the ceiling of their home. Furthermore, the bears make sure that the roof slopes upwards towards a hole at the back of the cave, ensuring that all the carbon dioxide makes its way out while they slumber. Stories like this had me in awe of the web of nature and how the range of wildlife had managed to survive and thrive.

Herds of elk and bison migrate at various times of the year on trails that stretch for hundreds of miles. Even in the snow these trails are visible. The national park ensures that these ancient trails are protected, with minimal roadways and disturbances. There is no doubt these creatures could not survive without the park, as it serves to protect an environment in which nature can live, die and procreate in as natural a home as is possible in this day and age.

A book I read recently spoke about the growth of the psychiatric treatment of animals. The point was being made that basically there was nothing wrong with the animals – their illness was caused by inappropriate environments. Being locked in an apartment all day, not sharing life with other animals and the limitations of zoos were causes of unhappiness in these creatures, for which they were now being medicated.

It doesn't take a large leap of the intellect to begin to wonder why so many people are on prescribed or even illegal drugs to help them deal with an increasingly hostile environment. Drugs were once described to me as 'reality-altering substances'. Reality is too hard, so I medicate, is the unconscious impulse of many today. Maybe there is a lesson to be learnt from the national parks – if creation is to flourish it requires the right environment.

Outside my cabin in Wyoming on a January day

#Nobility

In twelfth-century Paris, a young boy starts his first days at his apprenticeship. The roughness and toughness of the long days and the vagaries of the building site are new to him. He is finding it difficult and at times he wants to run home.

He wants to be a man – as his father asks of him – yet these new demands make him wonder if this challenge is beyond his reach or even his capabilities. His family are stonemasons, and they've come in from an outlying village to work for better wages, yet they hadn't reckoned with the cost-of-living increase in the urban setting. Neither had they realised how they took rural life for granted. The ready availability of produce without cost always eased their hunger and thirst.

The young boy looked at two of his uncles as they chiselled. One was gruff and angry, which led to numerous errors and mistakes, adding to the cost of materials and the ire of the foreman. Another uncle worked at a slower pace. Every blow was accurate and measured – he never appeared to break a sweat and always had time to nod or have a word with fellow workmates passing by.

Thinking that it was the assigned tasks that were the cause of the different expressions of personality, he ventured to ask each uncle what they were doing. He wanted to avoid the obviously frustrating job that the first uncle was assigned to.

In response to the question the first uncle replied, 'Are you stupid, don't you see I'm cutting stone?' and muttered unrepeatable words under his breath while shooing the young boy away. He asked the second uncle the same question. He replied with a smile as he looked skywards, 'I'm building a cathedral.'

We frequently talk about nobility and purpose, especially in organisations and in our workplace. Very often it is very difficult to say exactly what these things mean. All too often leadership can speak in riddles and jargon, which are greeted with ever-increasing apathy and serve only to contribute to lower morale. Regardless of circumstances or environment, we must nurture and safeguard our dignity and let no one steal it from us.

An unusual angle on the Spire and the Customs House in Dublin

#Pageantry

A few weeks ago, a friend of mine was stolen from us before his time. Though I am a priest and I celebrate many funerals, when someone I love dies it hurts. Apart from struggling to find the right things to say while leading the liturgy, one must bear personal grief with nobility and grace.

Watching the pageantry surrounding Queen Elizabeth's death in September 2022 brought home to me the power of ritual during times of loss. Whether it be a good friend, a family member or a head of state, the wisdom of the ages is often captured in dress, silent gatherings, slow walks, tunes of lament, and the well-chosen words that have been tried and tested over centuries.

A common request at many funerals today, be they religious or humanist, is that they celebrate a life. Sometimes that's all that's wanted. The celebration of a life may at times be easy to capture, as was the case with the late Queen Elizabeth. Her dedication to her role and her deep faith are lauded. Her cheerfulness and kindness are remembered. Reference was made to the difficult times in her life that she had to negotiate. However, there was also room for grieving, both public and private.

Some of the rituals in the pageantry gave room to people to say that they were hurting, whether it be for Her Majesty, or simply for 'Mummy' or 'Granny'. During the celebrations of her achievements, space was left to express the pain of it all. Furthermore, the cry 'the Queen is dead, long live the King' acknowledges that while many were in shock, the need to move on is ever present. We are even reminded in the rituals to pray for the grace we need as we face uncertain futures.

Regardless of our political persuasion or our personal views of royalty, the pageantry and ritual are well tested, and they do give us an occasion to reflect on own journeys through grief, loss and life. Yes, there is the need to celebrate lives, but there is also a need to create room and rituals that allow us to be sad, while also acknowledging the necessity of moving on. All these elements are present within my soul as I remember my great friend who passed away well before his time. Whatever stage of grief we are at as we remember those we love, we pray for the grace, expressed in the words of St John Henry Newman, 'Lead thou me on'.

A foal and her mother in County Longford, Ireland

Rabbits

Bull Island is a strip of sand that lies in Dublin Bay. It is surrounded by sea water and is home to an amazing range of wildlife and plants. It was a destination for many nature trips when we were young. I learned a lot from my teachers, enough to give me confidence to pursue my own studies as I grew older. One strong memory I have is of walking among the sand dunes, where I'd arrive at a relatively flat area that was alive with rabbits. No sooner did I appear than the rabbits disappeared into their burrows and the place emptied of life in a matter of seconds. On occasion, some of the smaller rabbits would run around, appearing a little lost, but they were never far behind their parents and would eventually find their way into the safety of a burrow.

Over time I developed the sense to hide behind one of the dunes, ensuring that the wind was blowing in my direction, so that my scent would not be picked up by the rabbits. Sure enough, after a short while a few heads would pop out of the burrows and immediately pop back in again until the braver among them would make their way out into the open spaces. Within minutes the place was alive again. They never stayed in their burrows for too long. There was an energy in them to get back out again and to do what they do best, filling the area with their fun and frolics and even the odd playful fight. Somehow, they managed to work around unwelcome interruptions.

There are occasions in life when we disappear into our own

burrows. Like the head coming over the dune, circumstances mean we must find a way to hide from the world, sometimes for our own safety, sometimes for that of others. Time becomes a healer, and we can find our way back into life again. There comes a time to stick our head out of our burrows again and do what we do best. There are many examples one can think of where this has happened to people in the past, particularly with those who experience God in new ways. Today, however, let's just think of times when you managed to pop your head out of a burrow and got back into the amazingness of life one more time.

Sunflowers on the deck of a friend's house

#Retreat

'Life begins at the edge of your comfort zone', or so says the writer Neal Donald Walsch. I think it's fair to say that I spent most of my childhood pushing myself outside my comfort zone. In an ordinary Dublin suburb, I climbed trees with friends – each one of us trying to outdo the other. I look at those trees now and a shiver runs down my spine. Ropes and clothes lines were tied together, creating a swing that allowed us to cross the river without need of a bridge! We also learned to develop that innocent look when mothers were wondering why all their clothes lines went missing at the same time! We built camps, often 'borrowing' timber from building sites. We made go-carts with timber and wheels from the many no-longer-needed prams, and then we found the biggest hill from which we could gain the fastest speed, only to discover the reason and purpose – all too late – for things called brakes!

These adventures taught me to be healthily suspicious of comfort zones and that there is great adventure beyond them. As we grow older, we can find ourselves becoming emotionally sterile and spiritually bored. The humdrum of our day-to-day dealings leaves us relying on comfort as the key outcome of life, and we become bored with our own existence.

For me, faith, in the religious sense, is not simply a time to give something up or to do a kindly deed or an inane spiritual exercise. It is a time to get out of my comfort zone and taste new frontiers and new ways of being. In short, time given to God is time that puts an end to boredom. It is time to climb and swing and to be adventurous with things of the soul. The spiritual journey looks beyond comfort zones and examines some of the existential realities of life. The end of Lent, for instance, is marked with many images, one of which is a large stone that is rolled back, shedding light on an area of life that was previously associated with the darkness of suffering and death. Take time regularly to spot a few stones that we need to roll back to let the light into stale places. Don't be afraid of naming a simple practice to get you out of your comfort zone – find that edge and plan to live again.

The Maine coastline

#Rituals

Papua New Guinea is a place that fills me with a certain curiosity. Over the years I've read books about what is the world's second largest island. There were many stories of tribes who lived isolated lives and remained disconnected from the outside world. One book that really interested me was by the travel writer Christina Dodwell, who spent two years exploring the country. She walked, canoed and rode a thousand miles on horseback, encountering people who had never even seen a horse before.

My interest in this country was reawakened recently when I was fortunate to stumble across an exhibition about the country's culture and traditions. I was intrigued by the tribal initiation ceremonies and other less formal gatherings through which tribes communicated. Cut off from the wider world, they relied on stories that were often integrated into songs and dances.

One of these initiation narratives lasts for twenty-one years! A long box set by any means. The story, as it unfolds, contains many of the responsibilities that fall on the head of a household throughout those years. What intrigued me most was that the story started with how you build a house and home. Cut off from the rest of the world, in the isolation of their tribe and culture, this community realised that if you are to build a secure life for yourself, and those who matter to you, a roof must go over your head.

These stories are often referred to as rituals, which have many objectives. They make the past present and help bring people closer to what is beyond, they bind people in community, and they focus on order and survival.

'Jerry' a legend in City Quay

River

I really enjoyed my time as a secondary school teacher. The school was quite close to Dublin's River Liffey, and on occasion I provoked the students by claiming that I could 'jump that river'. What followed then were howls of laughter and several colloquial adjectives suggesting that I had lost it. The cuter among them asked me to put my money where my mouth was and take a bet. A few times during the year, the school organised hikes in the Wicklow Mountains for the class groups. Before we'd park at our destination, I'd ask the driver to travel up the Military Road, getting him to pull in at a particular bog at the foot of Kippure. I'd bring the group across the short expanse of marshland and introduce them to the source of the River Liffey and, yes, you've guessed it – I'd jump across the narrow stream. I reminded them of my previous claim that I could 'jump' this river. Well, you should have seen the disappointment on the faces of those who were waiting for their payout.

When we'd go back into class after our trip to the mountains, I'd get the students to think about what had happened and how to make it from one river bank to the other as they progressed through their education. They'd find it hard to work it out at first, as some were so accustomed to disappointment that they never wanted to hope for anything. Using this experience, we'd look at what was achievable by setting smaller goals rather than thinking of things that were too far beyond their reach.

A short reflection on the biblical story of Jacob fording the river gave great encouragement. Certainly, moving to new places requires the sort of support and encouragement that Jacob received from the angel. A lot of chats started, and for many the angels were their grannies and grandads.

Sometimes these reflections on life's experiences taught the students more than a curriculum can contain. As Norman McClean said in his novel A *River Runs Through It* as he reflected on his life, 'At the time I did not know that stories of life are often more like rivers than books.'

The River Avon making its way through the city of Bath, England

#Road Back

Our personal history and the history of the world teaches us that coming out of difficult situations is not easy, whether we're dealing with grief, change of home, migration, pandemics, pestilences or just life in general. The epic Exodus adventure in the Bible teaches us this simple truth. Though slaves for years, many of those that were liberated experienced discontent when they experienced freedom in the desert. Some even wanted to go back into the comfortable structures of slavery. They craved the familiar routine of imprisonment and may have lost faith and the ability to have recourse to their rational and imaginative capabilities. Time in captivity and time spent in lockdown or in self-isolation, as we well know, can be a time of disempowerment.

The words of Ellis Reading from *The Shawshank Redemption* could be applied to the Exodus experience and to many other situations in life. Referring to prison life he said, 'These walls are funny. First you hate 'em. Then you get used to 'em. Enough time passes, you get so you depend on them. That's institutionalised.'

When we live carefree lives, we are unconsciously focused on and carried by the objectives of the organisations, communities and society that we are a part of. People in education, for the most part, focus on students. Members of faith groups concentrate on worship and building community together, members of sporting organisations aim to win and to support those who have the chance of glory.

However, personal and organisational challenges often require us to do something which for many is not natural. We are told to take the focus away from other objectives and focus on self and care for those immediate to us. We must stop thinking about other objectives and think of ourselves.

The way out of crisis and challenge is to realign ourselves with the objectives of the organisations of which we are a part. For instance, though the Covid-19 pandemic may be over, we can remain 'locked-in' in our thinking, as Ellis Reading so rightly observed. Christian faith encourages us always to reflect on 'the other', be that the mystery of God or our duty to our neighbour. The mystery of faith leads us from our preoccupied selves and helps us take bold and imaginative steps towards a world of neighbourliness, a community of care and of generosity for our neighbour. The call to humanity is not to dwell in isolation but to respond to a call into a deeper, more caring and mutually beneficial relationship with all that is.

The Samuel Beckett
Bridge in Dublin

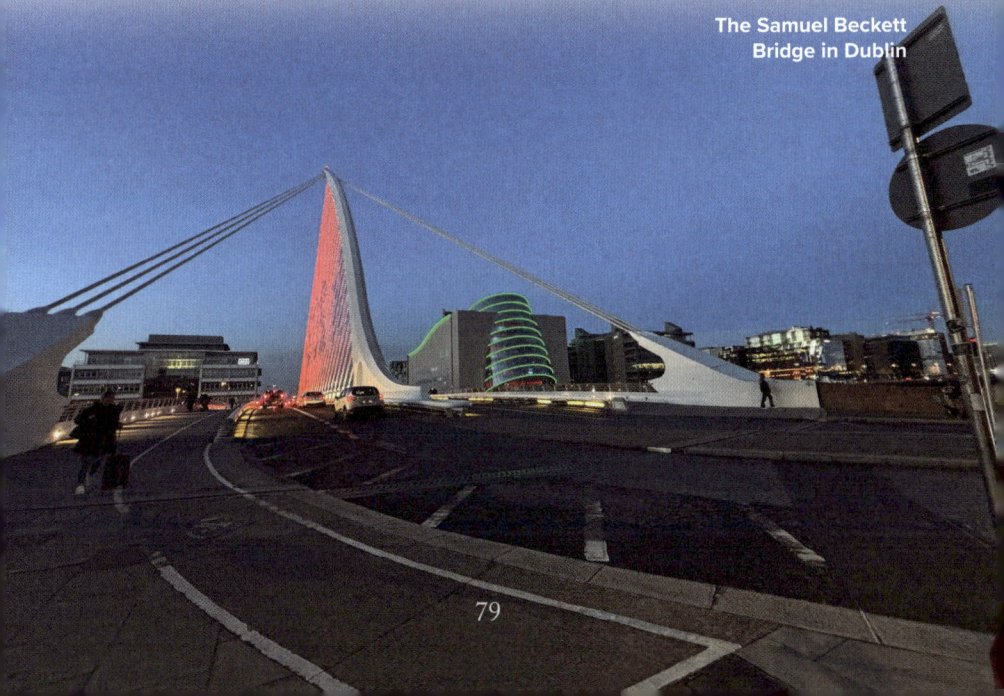

#Sabbatical

I was very fortunate to be able to take a sabbatical for a few months. It took me a while to get my head around it. First thing I had to do was to try to find out what a sabbatical was! When I looked it up, I noticed that the neo-liberal world we live in has stripped it down and has put its own suit of clothing on it. Now it is time off work to increase your skills so you can come back to work with a better productivity level!

Rather than get stuck into this very tight-fitting suit of clothes, I looked around a little more and found three biblical themes that provided some guidance. Firstly, in the Old Testament every seven years fields were left fallow – nothing was planted in them. Land cannot keep giving – it must replenish. People, like land, cannot keep giving. There must be a time to allow nature to do what it does best, and that is to replenish itself.

Secondly, Sabbath and hence sabbatical have a purpose. Most of us associate Sabbath with the commandment to keep it holy. This often translates into rushing to the church or the synagogue. The purpose of Sabbath was to give people a time in the week when they were not slaves. What is the point of being free if you don't take time to remember and celebrate? So many things enslave us, and we need to be free of them. I was speaking recently to someone whose child has a serious drug addiction. The spiral of violence and merciless debt collection is a modern form of slavery if ever there was one. If that family were free of this addiction and its accompanying trials, they would be forever grateful. Thirdly, and finally, Sabbath is a celebration of freedom – if we are lucky enough to be free. Heading off to worship is to give thanks for this freedom.

The key outcome, though, is to allow all these ideas and the time spent on sabbatical to percolate into every day from here on out. Former practices that were destructive must be banished and new life-giving ones embraced.

The lake at the University of Notre Dame in spring

#Silence

The Brandenburg Gate in Berlin instils emotion in me. Maybe you are old enough to remember the Berlin Wall being built, or those days in 1989 when it fell, and people clambered over the rubble to embrace a new-found freedom.

The gate has two two-storey buildings on either side of its large edifice. One houses a tourist information office, the other is home to 'the Room of Silence'. It's incredible that this symbol of political intrigue, turmoil and liberation offers a space where passers-by can enter and spend time in quiet contemplation.

A beautiful tapestry hangs on the room's walls. Initially it is hard to make out exactly what it represents but slowly, amid all the threads and lines, one begins to see young saplings in a forest reaching skywards. A trail through the centre of the trees leads to a bright sun, either setting or rising. Taking time to consider the tapestry, to find what it represents, is not unlike discovering silence within.

It's difficult to find silence these days – sometimes we'd love to just flick a switch and enter nirvana. Even on the bus, I often find myself having to put in earbuds to listen to some gentle music to block out all the frenetic conversations going on around me, whether it's people catching up with friends and loved ones around the world, or others sharing details of their everyday lives – what he said and she said, what I said and we said ...

However once found, it can be more difficult to know what to do with silence. The theologian and staunch resister of the Nazi dictatorship Dietrich Bonhoeffer said, 'In silence is embedded the marvellous power of clarification, purification and concentration on essentials'.

Quiet time – a few moments on a seat overlooking a beach or at the back of a church, a walk across a field or a long a river – is an opportunity to catch up with our deepest and often most neglected self.

Bonhoeffer's words tell us that silence is never a waste of time; rather it helps us to find our way, to get the right perspective and to recharge the batteries of the soul.

Buffalo resting with the Teton Range in the background

#Saints

'What's a martyr?' he asked me. I thought for a moment and cobbled together a theological response. I blurted it out. He looked unimpressed and hummed some nonsense and, as if he disapproved, he kept his eyes down, looking at nothing.

When eventually he lifted his head, he caught me straight in the eye and said, 'I think a martyr is somebody who has to live with a saint!' I was puzzled for a while, but when he smiled, I laughed. I got where he was coming from. I thought of all the people I knew who thought they had saintly status, and boy were they hard work. To live with them is indeed a form of martyrdom.

Saints, for me, are important. It's not the plaster statues that do it for me but their wisdom and legacy. There is not one problem I encounter, not one wall I can't see over, that one of the saints hasn't experienced too; they offer me a lifeline.

When I'm anxious or distressed, I think of the beautiful prayer of Teresa of Ávila, found after her death: 'Let nothing disturb you, let nothing frighten you, all things pass away.' It always brings me to a better place. Then there is St Francis of Assisi, who just wakes me up to delight in the beauty and wonder of creation. Francis's simple and peaceful mindset tells us that all things are our brothers and sisters and nothing can be destroyed or overlooked, just admired and rejoiced in. Then there are lesser-known saints like Peter Chanel. He spent his whole life on an island in the Pacific and, when he died, he had achieved nothing. However, following his death, people reflected on his existence, and they embraced his message. Sometimes I feel frustrated with a lack of results and outcomes. Peter inspires me not to become distracted and to keep focused on doing what is right and good.

There is a saint for everyone, and there is a saint for every day. For Christians, they are our family, and they are worth getting to know. And if you feel sainthood is not for you, remember that a saint is someone with a past, a sinner is someone with a future!

Walking in snow shoes in the Grand Teton Range

Soul

Black or white, right or left, light or darkness, right or wrong, pass or fail, good or bad. So much of our day is spent juggling these opposites in our head. Decisions about life, people, work, family and leisure are often struggles between extreme choices or outcomes. If they stayed in the brain that'd be okay, but usually an emotional tug accompanies these thoughts, bringing us into a good or bad space.

I read somewhere that because humans are focused on survival, three quarters of our brain activity is attending to things that can harm us. How often, when we sit down at night, does anything that could threaten us in the present moment or in the future come swirling into our minds, leaving us disconsolate or even depressed? In early civilisations it might have been wild animals or a neighbouring tribe that were sources of danger. Now it can be bills, banks, illness, loneliness or even a bothersome family member. To be hot-wired to protect ourselves and to watch for danger may mean that we need to work harder to occupy a less panic- or fear-driven space and to harvest the good that surrounds us.

The only way I can do that is to get out of my head. I find my soul is one place that is not a world of either/or but a world that accommodates all and sundry. Yes, there are moments in my life when my mind gets locked into one way of thinking. When this happens, I step back and let my soul find me and my life becomes liveable again. These moments permit me to say goodbye to thoughts that could destroy me. Even during the most horrific grief and loss, I find myself entering the room of my soul, where I can carry the pain of desolation and loss alongside the privilege and honour of love at the same time.

With God's grace I try to balance both within me rather than being overtaken by one or the other. I try to get out of that either/or broom cupboard and dust down the room of the soul. This space can be like a parent who effortlessly holds a wailing child in one arm and a laughing one in the other while getting on with the business of the day.

A shore on one of Killarney's lakes

#Victims

Dachau in Munich was the first concentration camp I ever visited. There were many things that shocked me about the place and remain with me to this very day. One of the most frightening things I learned was the camp was opened in March 1933, a good number of years before the Second World War started. While we associate 'death camps' with certain cohorts of people during the war, Dachau was opened to punish those who disagreed with the new political powers in Germany. All dysfunctional political systems have one characteristic: they must create necessary enemies who then have to be annihilated physically or morally to hide the harmful intentions of those in power.

Sometimes this takes the form of reckless murder or simply taking a person's good name or discrediting their humanity. So, too, those in power who have lost their mandate to govern often have to create these scenarios to prop up their faltering and unsavoury leadership, with catastrophic consequences for the innocent and the good.

During Holy Week we recount the story of a man who enters a city to the adulation of the crowd. In a short time, his presence results in upsetting those in power, he is labelled the enemy and becomes their victim. The theologian René Gerard said, 'In preventing a riot and dispersing a crowd, the crucifixion is an example of cathartic victimisation.'

Strangely enough, there is always a great silence after a crucifixion or a massacre. For those in power, after the crowds have gone home somewhat placated, they find the next victim so they can hold their crazy worldview together and so seek to appease the crowd again. This is not something new – it is a pattern of history.

What was new about the first Holy Week was that when Jesus faced his death God said I need no more victims – I don't need to be placated by anyone else's blood. I have learnt from this to try to speak kindly and to become more and more aware of all the forces at play that seek to dehumanise others in my mind and heart, whether it be in conversation, or on various media and social media platforms. Don't let them away with it – don't become like them. Whether you are a Christian or not, be less afraid of the enemies and more afraid of those who have created them.

Birkenau
Concentration
Camp

Willie Clancy Summer School

'Are you down for the week?' This is the most frequently asked question during the Scoil Samhraidh Willie Clancy (Willie Clancy Summer School) in Milltown Malbay, County Clare. It's the closest thing to a mating call for those who appear, year in and year out, at this most amazing festival. There are classes, sessions, concerts, lectures and céilidhs on the programme. There's no way that any single human being can keep up with it all. It is definitely not for the fainthearted, and it's not a normal timetable by any stretch of the imagination.

The preparations are made well in advance by thousands of people. Houses are in scarce supply but whatever is available is booked – it sleeps five but add a zero. Tents are dotted along the dunes and the occupants remain fearful of that inevitable night of gust, gale and downpour as canvas rips away from pole only to land in the next parish. The camper vans occupy precious locations and line up alongside one another, as if to have conversations about the eccentricities of their owners and drivers.

Those going to classes have packed their instruments and, depending on age, have clothed themselves to impress or to survive. You have people like Andy, who, having retired from a lifetime of banking, has decided to recreate himself as a musician at the tender age of fifty-seven. He sits in a class with people, most of whom are less than a quarter his age. They soak up the tunes, and, as he struggles to keep up with their sponge-like minds, he gets frustrated and depressed, realising that his brain has the absorption rate of a Brillo pad.

The dancers head off like clockwork to take up their familiar spaces on the floor so those on their dance list can find them. Everyone has their favourite dancers. There are those who move with ease to music and others who move to some bizarre tune in their heads that bears little relation to anything that the céilidh band is playing – surely a parable for life in general. Shirts, pre-sprayed with anti-perspirant, are changed after a good rub down with the not-too-attractive towel that hangs out of the back pocket.

Then there are the music sessions that start at lunchtime and go on and on and on until one o'clock the next morning or even the next day. It's disguised as music, but as sessions seek to draw tunes and souls together it knits together fibres of friendship that have unravelled with time. On occasion a neophyte arrives with a new bodhrán, bought in one of those shops in Dublin's O'Connell Street, one that's drier than the bonnet of a car in the Sahara. Quietly someone slips something into his hand, whispering, 'You'll get a sweeter tune if you use this.' Thinking they've received a compliment for their newfound talent, they open their bodhrán-playing hand to find they have been handed a very sharp steak knife!

The Bible tells us to clap and sing and dance and celebrate. There's nothing like good music and dancing to help the soul catch up with the body.

'Are you down for the week?'

'I am – sure isn't it great – even the walls are sweating!'

Acknowledgements

I'd like to extend my thanks to those at Messenger Publications, who encourage me to write, and to the team on RTÉ's *Rising Time*, who host 'A Word in Edgeways' and who keep me on my toes, especially the producer Sheila O'Callaghan, and to presenter Shay Byrne for his kind words, his warm humanity in the early hours of the morning and his amazing choices in music.

More from Alan Hilliard

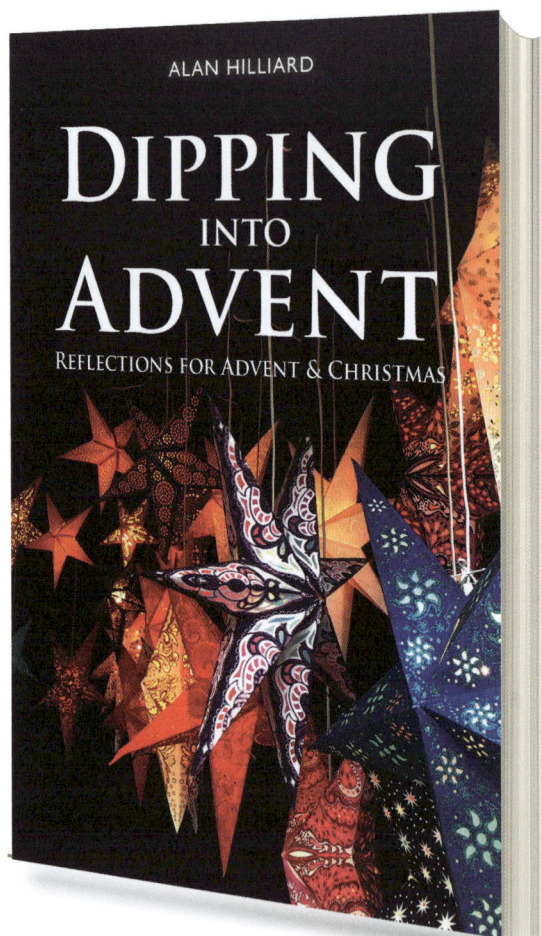

ALAN HILLIARD

DIPPING
INTO
ADVENT

REFLECTIONS FOR ADVENT & CHRISTMAS

Messenger MJP Publications

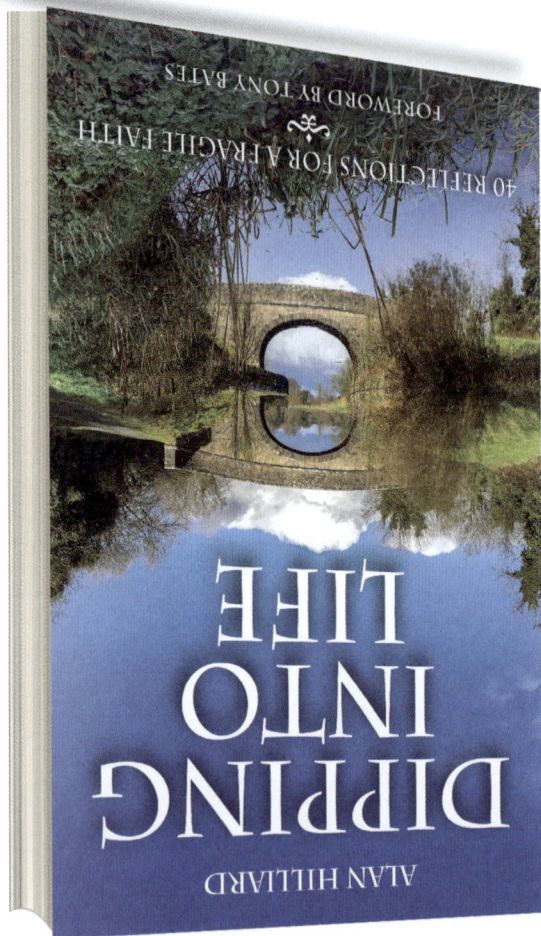

FOREWORD BY TONY BATES

40 REFLECTIONS FOR A FRAGILE FAITH

DIPPING INTO LIFE

ALAN HILLIARD

Also available from Messenger Publications, www.messenger.ie